Dolphins

By Elizabeth Allen

World Discovery Science Readers™

SCHOLASTIC INC.

New York • Toronto • London • Auckland • Sydney
Mexico City • New Delhi • Hong Kong • Buenos Aires

Atlantic spotted
dolphins

Chapter 1

What Is a Dolphin?

Imagine you are swimming in the ocean. A dark shadow moves toward you. It's a dolphin! The dolphin does not seem afraid. It watches you with curious eyes. It circles you and pokes you with its bony **beak**. It even lets you stroke its smooth skin.

Many people have had experiences just like this. Dolphins are wild animals, but they seem to like humans. Most humans like dolphins, too. The dolphin's friendly personality makes it one of the ocean's best-loved animals.

Some dolphins have curved mouths. They look as if they are smiling all the time.

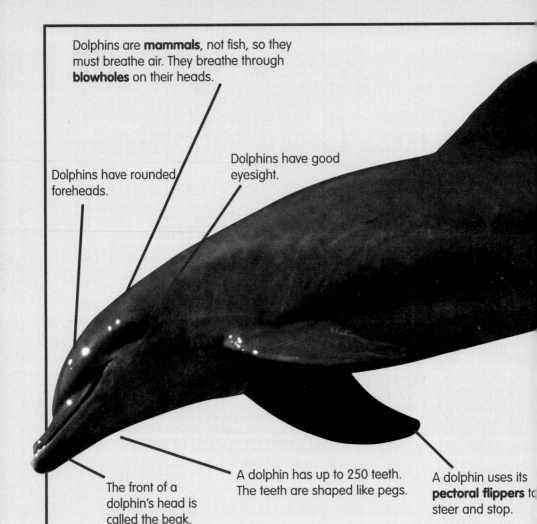

Dolphins are **mammals**, not fish, so they must breathe air. They breathe through **blowholes** on their heads.

Dolphins have rounded foreheads.

Dolphins have good eyesight.

The front of a dolphin's head is called the beak. The beak includes the mouth.

A dolphin has up to 250 teeth. The teeth are shaped like pegs.

A dolphin uses its **pectoral flippers** to steer and stop.

There are more than forty species of dolphins. Different species have different features, but all dolphins have some things in common. The picture above shows the main parts of a dolphin's body.

The **dorsal fin** keeps a dolphin steady as it swims.

A dolphin's skin feels smooth. It is very sensitive to touch.

A dolphin's tail is flat. It has two parts called **flukes**.

Dolphins have bones inside their pectoral flippers. The bones look similar to the hands or feet of a land animal.

Dolphins come in many different sizes and colors. These differences help us to tell species apart.

The biggest dolphin is the orca. The orca is also called the killer whale, but it is really a dolphin. The "killer" part of the name comes from the fact that these dolphins are powerful and fierce hunters. The "whale" part comes from the orca's large size. Male orcas can be up to 32 feet (9.8 m) long and may weigh 22,000 pounds (10,000 kg). Female orcas can be up to 28 feet (8.5 m) long and may weigh 16,500 pounds (7,500 kg). Orcas have bold black-and-white skin patterns.

Orcas

Comparing Dolphins

Species	MAXIMUM Length	MAXIMUM Weight
Orca	19-22 feet (5.8-6.7 m)	8,000-12,000 pounds (3,600-5,400 kg)
Bottlenose	8.5 feet (2.6 m)	440 pounds (200 kg)
Common	6.5 feet (2 m)	165 pounds (75 kg)
Striped	7.5 feet (2.3 m)	220 pounds (100 kg)
Spinner	6 feet (1.8 m)	165 pounds (75 kg)
Spotted	6.9 feet (2.1 m)	200 pounds (90 kg)

There are several small dolphin species. The black dolphin, which lives near Chile, is only about 5 feet (1.5 m) long. The Hector's dolphin of New Zealand also measures about 5 feet (1.5 m) from nose to tail. Both species weigh between 110 and 130 pounds (50 and 60 kg).

The spotted dolphin is a medium-sized species. It can grow up to 8 feet (2.4 m) long and may weigh 250 pounds (115 kg). Spotted dolphins are dark gray on top with lighter bellies. They are sprinkled with white or gray spots.

Dolphins can be found all over the world. Any time you are near the ocean, there is a chance that you might spot one of these amazing animals!

Some dolphins like cold water. Hourglass dolphins and southern rightwhale dolphins live near the Antarctic. White-beaked dolphins live in the upper North Atlantic, near the Arctic Circle.

Other dolphins prefer warm water. Striped dolphins, spotted dolphins, spinner dolphins, and many other species stick to warm seas.

Hourglass dolphin in the south Atlantic Ocean

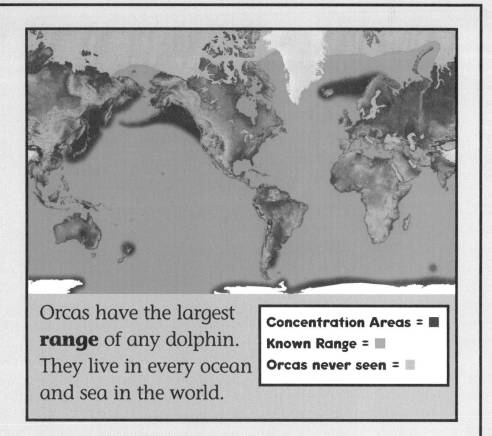

Orcas have the largest **range** of any dolphin. They live in every ocean and sea in the world.

Concentration Areas = ■
Known Range = ■
Orcas never seen = ■

Different dolphins also prefer different water depths. Some dolphins live only near coasts. Others live out at sea. Some species, such as common dolphins, can be found in both places.

Common dolphins

Dolphins lob-tailing

Chapter 2

A Dolphin's Life

Nellie, the oldest known dolphin, lives in a marine park in Florida. Nellie turned fifty years old in February 2003. Scientists believe some wild dolphins might be even older.

A dolphin does many things during its long lifetime. It is born and it grows up. It travels and plays. It learns to communicate with other dolphins, and it hunts for food.

A dusky dolphin breaching near New Zealand

Dolphin Behavior

Here are some of the things dolphins often do in the wild:

Spy-hopping	Poking the head out of the water to look around.
Lob-tailing	Smacking the flukes on the water's surface.
Flipper slapping	Smacking the fins or flippers on the water's surface.
Breaching	Leaping out of the water.

Baby dolphins depend on their mothers for food, protection, and much more. They stay near their mothers for the first two years of their lives.

A newborn dolphin is small and weak. It has no teeth, and its dorsal fin and tail flukes are soft and floppy. The mother dolphin pushes her baby to the water's surface to take its first breath of air. She protects the baby from anything that might hurt it.

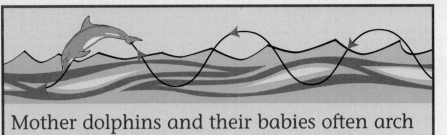

Mother dolphins and their babies often arch in and out of the water as they travel. This is called **porpoising**.

Baby dolphins live on their mother's milk at first. After a few months, their teeth start to grow. Then they can eat fish, squid, and other grown-up food. But babies still keep drinking some milk until they are about two years old.

A Indo-Pacific humpbacked dolphin mother and calf near Hong Kong. Calves are born almost black. This color gradually fades to pink or white as the calf matures.

   Dolphins are social animals, which means they like to be together. They live in groups called **pods**. Pod sizes are different from species to species. Some dolphins form small pods with just a few members, while other dolphins will live in pods of 30 individuals or more. Sometimes many pods of dolphins will temporarily come together to form huge herds with thousands of members. Sailors often see these enormous dolphin groups far out at sea.

Pod members are usually friendly with one another. They swim close together and touch one another with their flippers and flukes. They also play tag and leap out of the water together. Sometimes two pod members become close friends and stick together throughout their lives.

Dolphins sometimes fight. They scratch each other with their teeth and leave lines on each other's skin. These lines are called **rake marks**.

Sounds are very important in a dolphin's everyday life. Dolphins use sound to communicate and to learn about their environment.

Dolphin "talk" sounds like squeals, clicks, and whistles. A dolphin makes these noises with air sacs inside its head. Other dolphins can tell whether the sounds mean danger is near or food has been found. They can even recognize other dolphins by the sounds they make.

The **melon** is a fat-filled organ inside the dolphin's forehead. Sounds leave the dolphin's body through the melon.

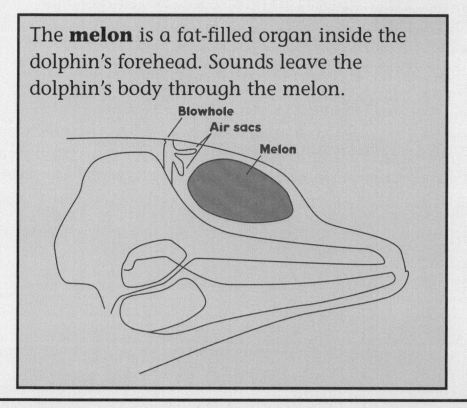

Blowhole
Air sacs
Melon

Dolphins also use sound to "see" things. Clicks from their air sacs travel forward into the water. The sound bounces off things

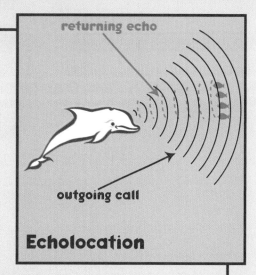

returning echo

outgoing call

Echolocation

and returns to the dolphin as echoes. The dolphin can tell what lies ahead just by listening to the echoes. This process is called **echolocation**.

Atlantic spotted dolphin near the Bahamas, using echolocation to find fish buried in the sand at the bottom of the ocean

Long-beaked common dolphins preying on a trapped school of sardines near South Africa

Dolphins are predators, which means they eat other animals. Dolphins like to eat fish, squid, and jellyfish. Sometimes they also eat shrimp, clams, and other animals that live on the ocean floor.

Dolphins use echolocation when they hunt. They send sound beams ahead of them as they swim. They listen for echoes that tell them food is near. A dolphin can use echolation to sense prey that is too far away to see.

Pod members often hunt together. They spread out while they look for food. They call to one another when they find a school of fish or another tasty meal. All the dolphins swim over and surround the **prey**. Then they take turns grabbing and swallowing the trapped animals.

Dolphins tear prey apart with their teeth. They use their large tongues to push food into their throats.

Pacific white-sided dolphin

A pod of Atlantic spotted dolphins near the Bahamas in the Atlantic Ocean

Chapter 3

Learning About Dolphins

Many scientists want to learn more about dolphins. But it is hard to study these animals in the wild. For this reason, many aquariums around the world keep dolphins. **Captive** dolphins help scientists to learn about dolphin intelligence, communication, learning, and much more.

Aquariums are also a great place for the public to see dolphins in action. Anyone can visit and enjoy these incredible animals!

Performing dolphins leap high into the air, jump through hoops, do flips, toss balls, wave good-bye with their flippers, "talk" on command, and do many other amazing things.

Scientists have learned that dolphins have many incredible abilities. For instance, today we know that dolphins have amazing communication skills. Scientists at one aquarium taught dolphins a sign language that had about fifty simple words like "hoop," "ball," and "bring." The scientists combined the words to make phrases. The dolphins proved that they understood the phrases by following every command perfectly.

Get Ball

Toss Ball

Touch Beak (Nose)

Trainers use hand signals to tell dolphins what to do. Here are some signals a trainer might use.

Children learn about the anatomy of a captive dolphin in a class in Hawaii.

Dolphins also have very good social skills. Captive dolphins form strong bonds with one another. They also become friends with their trainers, and they do not mind if friendly human strangers enter their tanks. Some marine parks even let visitors swim with the dolphins.

Most scientists believe that dolphins are very smart. They are studying captive dolphins to learn more about dolphin **intelligence**.

What are the signs of dolphin intelligence? There are many. Dolphins learn very quickly compared to other animals. Sometimes they even learn hard tricks just by watching one another! They communicate well with one another and with humans. They can solve simple problems, like finding their way through mazes. They can recognize themselves in mirrors, and they are very playful. Playfulness is thought to be a sign of intelligence.

Captive dolphins with their trainer

Dolphins also have big brains compared to the rest of their bodies. Only humans and chimpanzees have bigger brains. Some scientists think brain size is an important part of intelligence. If this is true, then dolphins might be some of the smartest animals on Earth!

Bottlenose dolphin playing with a child at a public aquarium in France

Dolphins and humans both have wrinkled brain surfaces. Some scientists think wrinkled brains are a sign of intelligence.

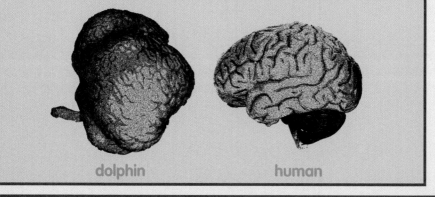

dolphin   human

Orca

Chapter 4

Dolphins in Danger

Dolphins are big and strong compared to most other ocean animals. Small animals usually stay away from larger animals, so dolphins are seldom attacked. But this does not mean that dolphins are safe all the time. The sea is a dangerous place, and sometimes dolphins run into trouble.

What threats do dolphins face?

Endangered Dolphins

Several dolphin species are either endangered or threatened. This means these species are in danger of dying out. This chart shows species that scientists are most worried about.

Name	Population
Baiji dolphin [Yangtze dolphin]	fewer than 100
Hector's dolphin [Maui's dolphin]	about 100
Indus River dolphin	about 1000
Ganges River dolphin	more than 4,000

Big predators sometimes find and attack dolphins. Large sharks such as great whites and tiger sharks like to eat dolphins. Orcas also eat smaller dolphins, even though they are dolphins themselves.

Sharks and orcas do not usually attack healthy adult dolphins. They go after dolphins that are very young, old, or sick. Why? These dolphins are weak, and they cannot defend themselves well.

Sometimes dolphins work together to drive predators away. A pod of dolphins will surround a shark. They then take turns ramming the shark with their pointed beaks. They continue until the shark gives up and swims away.

A dolphin bumping a nurse shark in the Caribbean Sea

Hawaiian spinner dolphin with wound from cookie cutter shark near the Hawaiian Islands

Imagine you see a dorsal fin poking out of the water. Is it a shark or a dolphin? A triangular fin probably belongs to a shark. A curvy fin probably belongs to a dolphin.

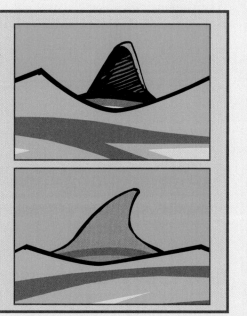

The U.S. government uses this symbol on some products. It means that dolphins were not harmed when the product was made.

U.S. Department of Commerce
Dolphin Safe

Humans are the dolphin's biggest enemy. The fishing industry kills hundreds of thousands of dolphins every year. Many dolphins die after they get tangled in drifting nets. Many others are caught by people fishing for tuna. Dolphins and tuna often swim together, so these animals may be netted at the same time. People usually release any living dolphins they catch. But the dolphins often drown before they can be released. The tuna-fishing industry is large, so this is a serious problem for world dolphin populations.

Some countries have fishing laws that protect dolphins. In many places, people are not allowed to use fishing nets above a certain size. Laws also tell people how many dolphins they are allowed to catch each year.

Laws like these have been a big help. Fewer dolphins are killed today than in past years. A few dolphin species are endangered, but most are not. The world's oceans are still full of these amazing and beautiful animals.

Atlantic bottlenose dolphin

Glossary

Beak: The pointy front of a dolphin's head.

Blowhole: A hole on top of a dolphin's head. Dolphins breathe air through these holes.

Breaching: Leaping out of the water.

Captive: Kept in a man-made environment, such as an aquarium.

Dorsal fin: The fin on a dolphin's back.

Echolocation: The use of sound and echoes to gather information.

Flipper slapping: Smacking the pectoral fins, or flippers, on the water's surface.

Flukes: The two flat halves of a dolphin's tail.

Intelligence: Mental ability.

Lob-tailing: Smacking the flukes on the water's surface.

Mammal: An animal that has warm blood and produces milk for its young.

Melon: A fatty organ inside a dolphin's forehead.

Pectoral flippers: The two flippers on a dolphin's underside.

Pod: A group of dolphins that lives and travels together.

Porpoising: Arching in and out of the water during travel.

Predator: An animal that hunts and eats other animals.

Prey: Any animal that is hunted by a predator.

Rake marks: Teeth marks on a dolphin's skin.

Range: All the areas where a type of dolphin may be found.

Species: A distinct type of living thing.

Spy-hopping: Poking the head out of the water to look around.